Planets

Venus

Dash!
LEVELED READERS
3

An Imprint of Abdo Zoom • abdobooks.com

Dash! LEVELED READERS

Level 1 – Beginning
Short and simple sentences with familiar words or patterns for children who are beginning to understand how letters and sounds go together.

Level 2 – Emerging
Longer words and sentences with more complex language patterns for readers who are practicing common words and letter sounds.

Level 3 – Transitional
More developed language and vocabulary for readers who are becoming more independent.

abdobooks.com

Published by Abdo Zoom, a division of ABDO, PO Box 398166, Minneapolis, Minnesota 55439.

Printed in the United States of America, North Mankato, Minnesota.
092018
012019

Photo Credits: iStock, NASA, Science Source, Shutterstock
Production Contributors: Kenny Abdo, Jennie Forsberg, Grace Hansen, John Hansen
Design Contributors: Dorothy Toth, Neil Klinepier

Library of Congress Control Number: 2018946188

Publisher's Cataloging in Publication Data

Names: Murray, Julie, author.
Title: Venus / by Julie Murray.
Description: Minneapolis, Minnesota : Abdo Zoom, 2019 | Series: Planets | Includes online resources and index.
Identifiers: ISBN 9781532125331 (lib. bdg.) | ISBN 9781641856782 (pbk) | ISBN 9781532126352 (ebook) | ISBN 9781532126864 (Read-to-me ebook)
Subjects: LCSH: Venus (Planet)--Juvenile literature. | Venus (Planet)--Observations--Juvenile literature. | Planets--Juvenile literature. | Solar system--Juvenile literature.
Classification: DDC 523.42--dc23

THIS BOOK CONTAINS RECYCLED MATERIALS

Table of Contents

Venus

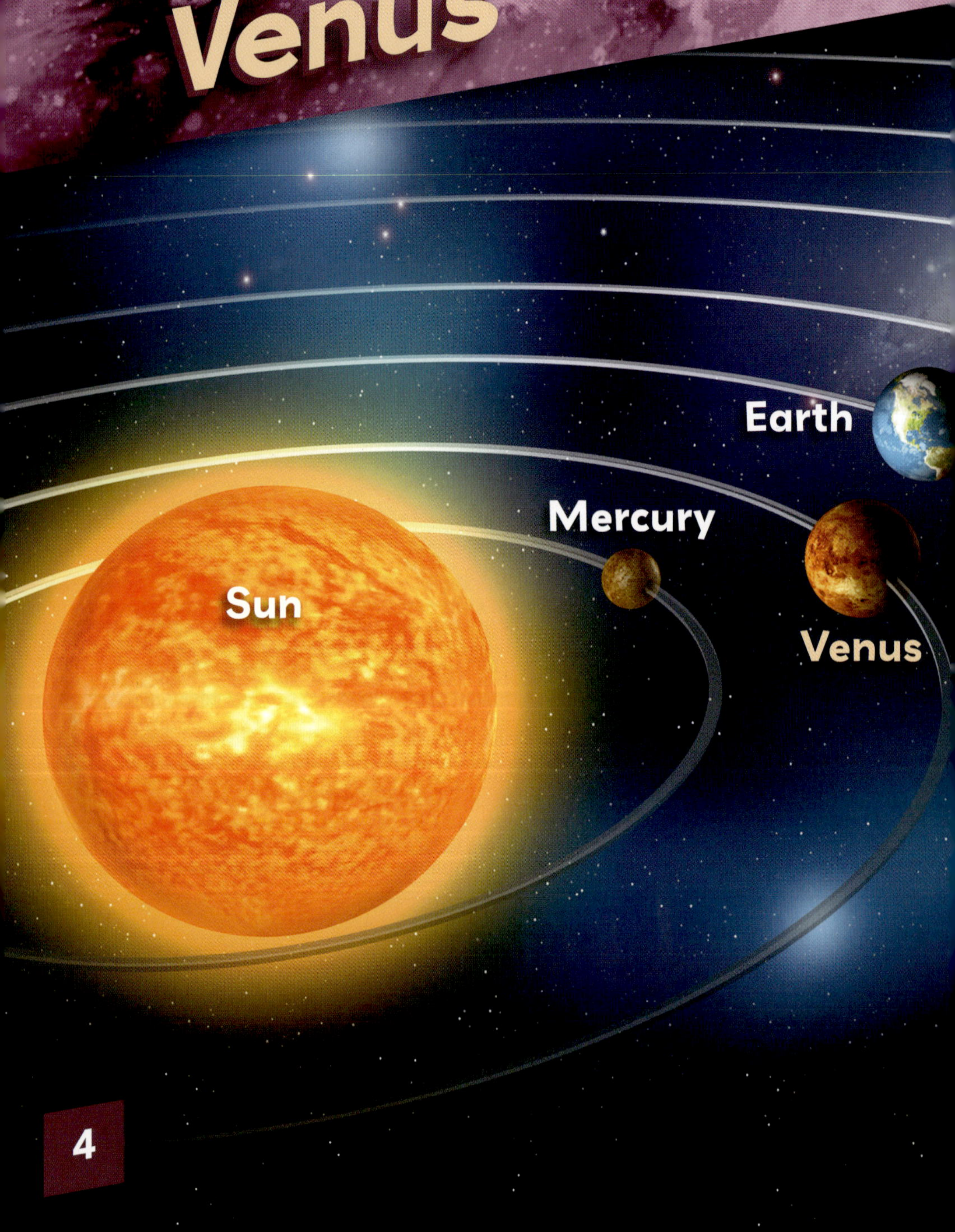

Venus is the second planet from the sun. It is the third-smallest planet. Venus has no moons or rings.

Venus is often called the Earth's "sister planet." It is the closest planet to Earth. It is the second brightest object in our night sky. Venus is also about the same size as Earth.

Venus **orbits** the sun every 225 Earth days. It spins very slowly as it orbits. It takes 243 Earth days to complete one rotation. That is a very long day!

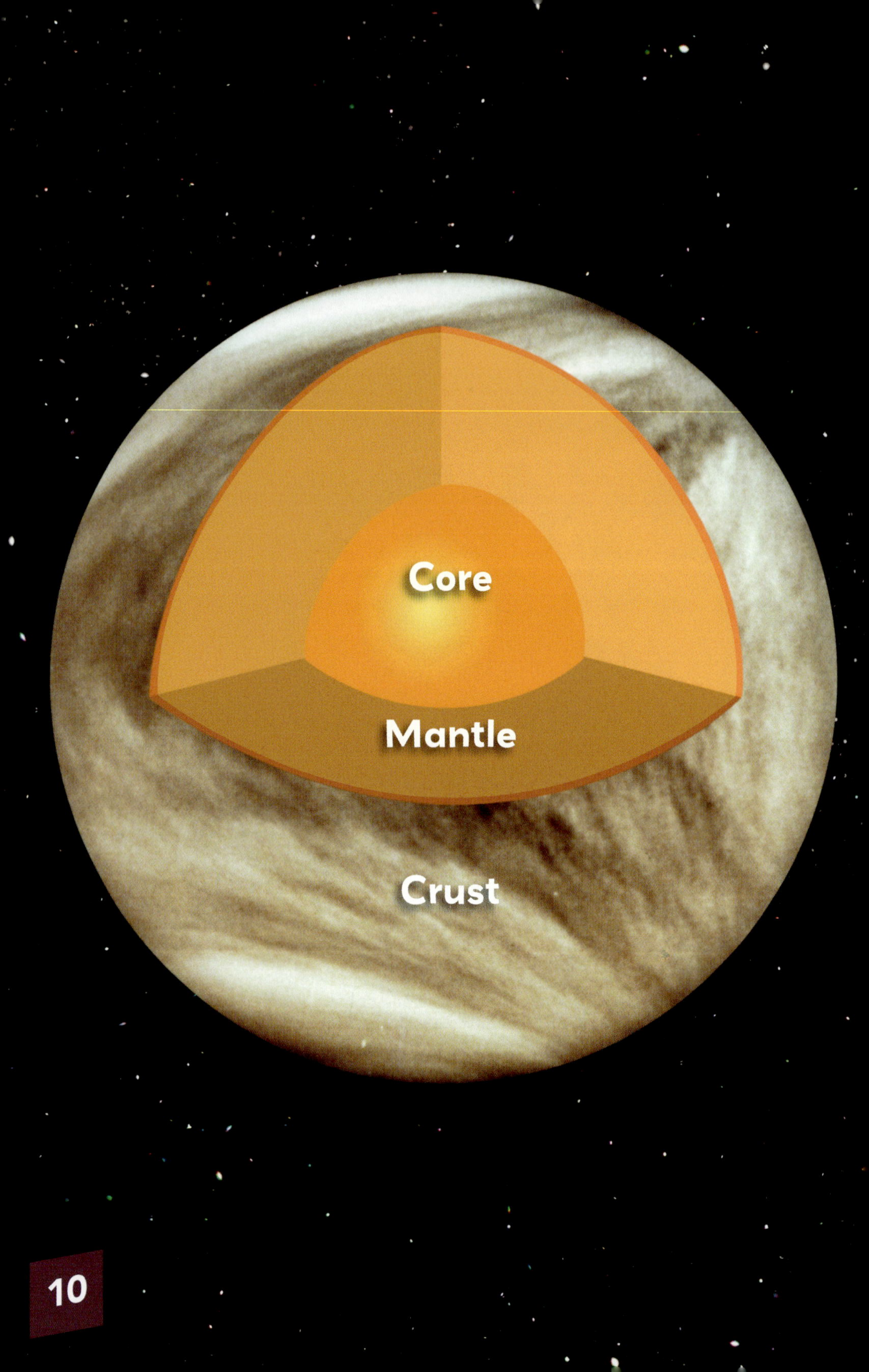
Core
Mantle
Crust

Venus has three layers. The inner core is mostly made up of iron. The mantle consists of hot, melted rock. The crust is the planet's outer layer.

Venus is a rocky planet. It has more than 1,600 giant volcanoes. It also has large craters and sand dunes.

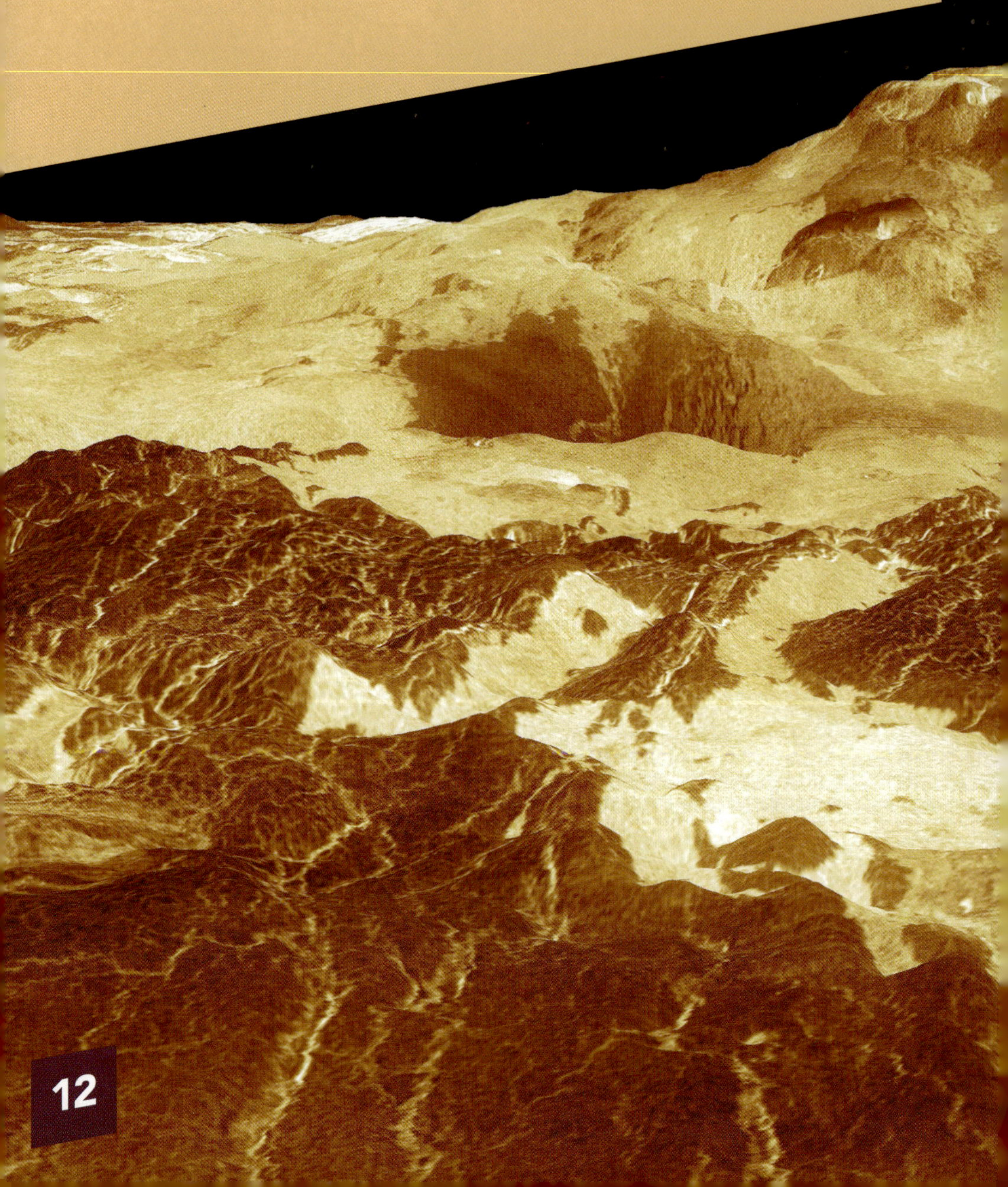

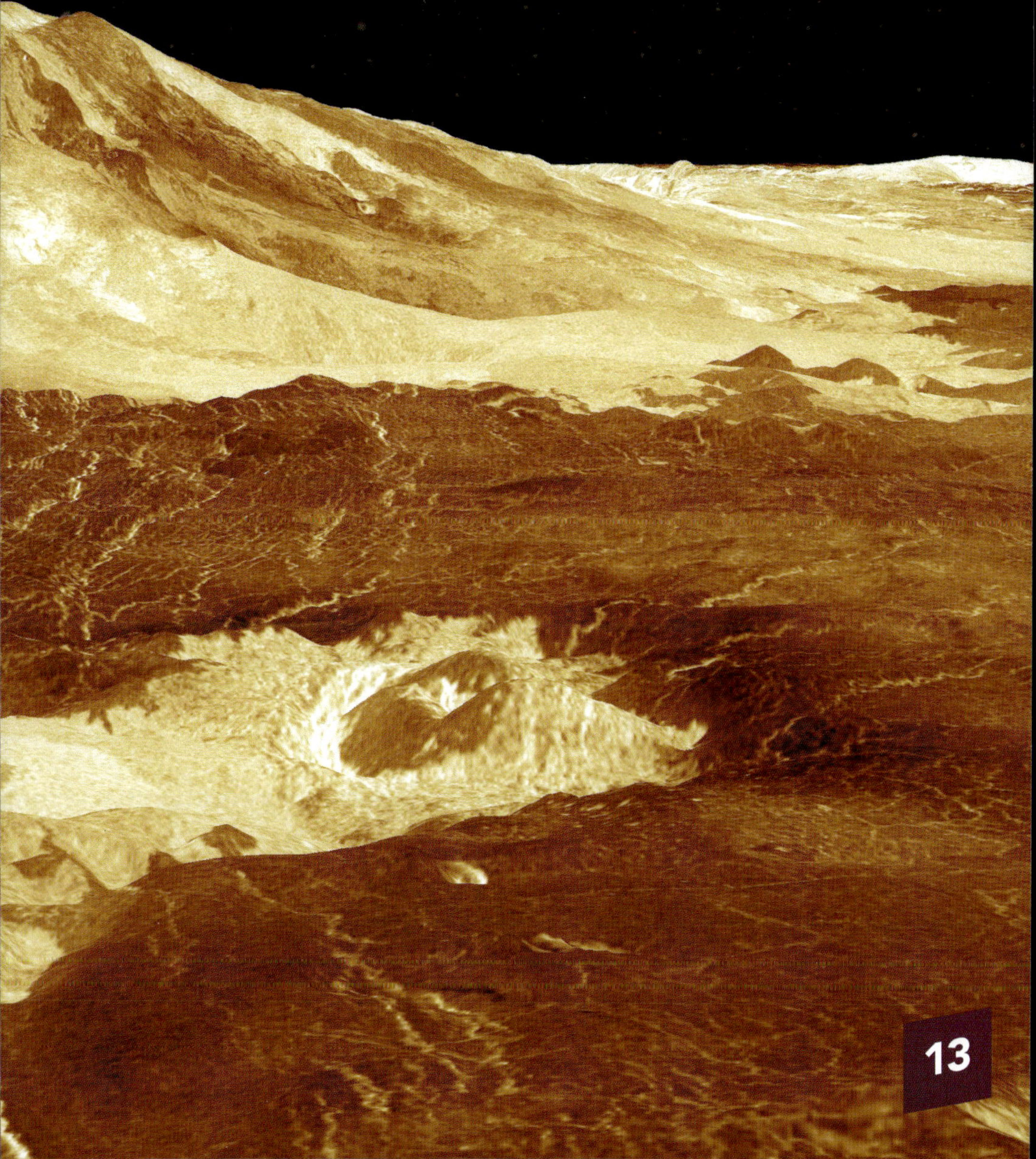

Thick Atmosphere

The **atmosphere** on Venus is thick and heavy. It is mainly made up of carbon dioxide. The pressure on Venus is so great that it would instantly crush a human.

Thick clouds surround Venus. These clouds trap the heat. Temperatures on Venus can reach 870 °F (465 °C). This makes it the hottest planet!

Missions to Venus

In 1962, Mariner 2 was the first spacecraft to fly by Venus. The Magellan **probe** mapped the entire surface of Venus in 1989.

USA

NASA and Russia are planning a joint mission to Venus. There is still much to learn about the planet, like if it once had oceans and life. The Venera-D **probe** hopes to launch in 2026.

SSRMS
P: 139.7 T: 58.4
F: 1841 I: 6.0
10 PRINT TAB(33);"LUNAR"
00:02:33
PET
Attitude
Y -179.46
P -0.07
R -0.06
Pri Snsr
CP to GF
Pos
Y 3.49
Z 34.27
VV to ISS
Pri 47.23
Sec 2.06

More Facts

- Maxwell Montes is the highest mountain on Venus. It is 7 miles (11.3 m) tall!

- Venus spins in a different direction than it **orbits**. This makes the sun rise in the west and set in the east on Venus.

- It takes 6 minutes for sunlight to reach Venus. This is because it is 67 million miles (108 million km) from the sun.

Glossary

atmosphere – the gases surrounding the earth or other planets in our solar system.

NASA – short for National Aeronautics Space Administration.

orbit – a curved path in which a planet, or other space object, moves in a circle around another body.

probe – an unmanned, exploratory spacecraft designed to transmit information about its environment.

solar system – a system that includes a star (the sun) and all of the matter which orbits it, including planets and their moons.

Index

Online Resources

Booklinks
NONFICTION NETWORK
FREE! ONLINE NONFICTION RESOURCES

To learn more about Venus, please visit **abdobooklinks.com**. These links are routinely monitored and updated to provide the most current information available.